Mem

D0561980

TWEEN YOU & ME

A Preteen Guide
to Becoming Your Best Self

created by

DEB DUNHAM

Empowerment Publishing
a Wyatt-MacKenzie Imprint

DEDICATION

This book is dedicated to my three children, Emily, Ben, and Olivia, who teach me how to be a conscious mother. Thank you for granting me unlimited love and forgiveness as I learn.

To Tim, my husband and friend, whose black and white view of the world helps me to see in full color. Thank you for believing in me. Your unique brand of support suits me perfectly.

Tween You and Me
A Preteen Guide to Becoming Your Best Self
by Deb Dunham

ALL RIGHTS RESERVED
©2009 by Deb Dunham
ISBN: 978-0-9820518-5-6
Library of Congress Control Number: 2009928159

Author Photo: Amanda Ambrose

Empowerment Publishing
a Wyatt-MacKenzie Imprint

For Imprint information visit: www.WyMacPublishing.com

Requests for permission or further information should be addressed to:
Wyatt-MacKenzie Publishing, 15115 Highway 36,
Deadwood, Oregon 97430

CONTENTS

CHAPTER 4 Feelings About My Life and the World

APPENDICES

PREFACE

Dear Tween,

Have you ever felt as if you are all alone and that no one understands the way you feel? Do you sometimes worry that you don't fit in? Do you ever feel impatient to grow up?

If you answered yes to any of these questions, this is the book that can help. Each page discusses a different feeling, or challenge, followed by a positive statement to help you change your thoughts.

By repeating these words out loud to yourself, maybe even while looking in a mirror, you will begin to see that when you change your thoughts, you change the way you feel about yourself and your life. With these new, positive statements you'll be able to become the best *you* there is. You are the most important person in your life. You deserve to feel great about you!

Deb Dunham

FOREWORD

Being a tween isn't easy. I make a lot of mistakes. And it can be scary thinking about becoming a teenager. But at the same time, having more responsibilities can be fun. As I become older, I feel more respected. Maybe I even respect myself more.

Tween You and Me is a great book. The ideas have helped me become stronger in tough situations. I can relate to a lot of the topics. It helps me to know that I'm not the only one who feels the way I do.

I have used the positive self-talk in this book. Being mean to myself doesn't help anything. But being positive does. Being positive helps you feel better. And that's important.

My advice to other tweens:

1. Read this book. It will help you.

2. Talk to your parents or another adult you trust. Every tween needs someone they can talk to.

3. Be happy and stay true to yourself no matter what.

Enjoy this book!
Emily Dunham
The Author's Now-Teenage Daughter

INTRODUCTION

Understanding Feelings and Thoughts

By the age you are now, you've learned lots of ways to care for your physical self—your body. You know about eating well, sleeping enough, keeping clean, and exercising. But you may not have learned about taking care of your emotional self—your feelings. Feelings are as much a part of you as the parts of your body that you can see. Feelings are important because they tell you what's going on inside your mind. They tell you what you want and need. So it makes sense to pay attention to your feelings.

All feelings are normal. Yes, all of them! There is no feeling you could ever have that makes you abnormal. And, just as your body needs exercise to be healthy, your feelings need to be exercised also. Your job is to learn how and when to express your feelings in healthy ways and at the appropriate time and place. This book will give you some suggestions about how to do that.

Imagine that your feelings are teachers. You naturally like some teachers better than others, and you probably like some feelings better, too. But it is best if you listen to all of them because they all have lessons for you.

So where do feelings come from anyway? Your feelings are created by the thoughts you choose. For example, if you think a movie is scary, you feel scared. If you think your day is going to be fun, you feel excited. You can see that since you are in control of your thinking, you control your feelings, too.

Now imagine that your thoughts are like magnets. The kinds of thoughts you think about are the kinds of feelings that are pulled toward you. This is true for the thoughts you have about yourself. Your thoughts have the power to help you or hurt you. So, the way you think about yourself and the way you talk to yourself really matters.

Every person has a conversation going on inside her head regularly. Often, the conversation is not nice.

Deb Dunham

You might say things to yourself that resemble bullying. When you make negative statements like, "I'm so dumb. I'm ugly. No one likes me. I can't do it," your body and mind feel bullied and become weaker. Try saying these negative things to yourself now while you pay attention to your body. How do you feel inside? Do you feel like someone has knocked you down? That's because your body hears and feels everything you say.

On the other hand, when you tell yourself thoughts of love and acceptance with words like, "I'm attractive. I like me. I'm a good person. I can do it," you pull in more pleasant feelings and experiences to yourself. You'll feel happier, stronger, and better about your life. Repeat the following words to yourself now and focus on how you feel: "I choose to love myself today in every way." Did you feel a boost? Did you start to smile?

As you read this book you will have lots of chances to practice listening to your thoughts, expressing your feelings, and using positive self-talk. If you aren't used to speaking nicely about yourself, it may feel strange at first. You may not even believe the positive words you say. Be patient and practice. This is a new way of caring for yourself. Like anything you learn that's new, positive self-talk will get easier if you keep at it.

You don't have to use only the words in this book. Make up your own phrases that feel good to you. One good thought usually leads to another. Before long you'll notice that feeling good about yourself is just a thought away. If you want to feel great about yourself, start now. You don't have to wait for other people to tell you how great you are, because you can tell yourself. So silence the bully in your head, and give the cheerleader a megaphone! You're awesome!

CHAPTER 1
Feelings about Myself

Sometimes I feel ugly. I wish I looked different.

Criticizing your appearance is like hitting yourself with an invisible hammer. Ouch! Yet many people do it regularly. Listen to the cruel things you say to yourself. Would you say these things to a good friend? Probably not. So start saying and doing the nice things for yourself that you'd do for a friend. You deserve your own best treatment.

Do you realize that even the happiest, most confident, and best-looking people that you know struggle with the desire to change something about themselves? It's not always easy to love yourself when the world tricks you into believing that you're not good enough. The truth is, you're more than good enough!

Did you know that pictures of models in magazines are always touched up and can completely change the way a person looks by covering up pimples, changing eye color, and even changing body shapes? Companies show you unrealistic pictures like this for one reason—to get you to buy their products like makeup, clothes, or skin cream. If you're still not convinced, take a look around you. Do you see anyone who looks like she stepped out of a magazine?

Here's a secret that everyone needs to know: the most attractive people are those who are comfortable in their own bodies. When you honor your natural beauty the world sees it, too. Try this: look in a mirror and put yourself down. Think of yourself as weak, ugly, dumb, and not good enough. Let your body show these feelings with sagging shoulders, a drooping head, and a pouting face. Yuck!

Deb Dunham

Now erase that image and look in the mirror again while building yourself up. Remind yourself that you are perfect as you are. You are talented, confident, and lovable. You feel great! Your body is up tall, your face is bright, and your eyes sparkle. Wow! What a difference. Remember that others can see the best you when you see the best you.

If you really think about it, our uniqueness—our differences—make the world an awesome and interesting place. Resist the urge to look like someone else and spend more time wanting to be you. The world thanks you.

Repeat these words:
I am now willing to accept
that I am okay
just as I am.

I have decided to accept
and appreciate
my body.
When I choose to love
myself, I see my
own beauty.

Sometimes I get so angry that I want to hit somebody or throw something.

Anger is a powerful emotion. It can easily grow out of control if you let it. When you're angry, you may not even recognize yourself. You might feel like a strange monster has jumped into your body.

While it's important to express how you feel, it's up to you to express yourself in a safe way. If you feel you may hurt yourself or others when you're angry, put up an imaginary stop sign in front of you, then walk away from the situation until you have calmed down. Try taking deep breaths or screaming into a pillow if that helps. Count backwards from ten as many times as it takes for you to feel calmer.

Another trick is to write, say, or draw the angry words you feel. You could even write a letter to the person you're angry with to release your harsh words, and then throw the letter away without sending it. This will let the anger out without hurting anyone.

When you're calmer, express how you feel without blame. Start your sentences with, "I feel…" instead of "You make me…" By approaching people in this way and taking responsibility for the anger that you feel, you make it easier for other people to understand you and for them to want to work out a solution with you.

Lastly, try not to be frightened of anger. Anger is just another emotion, one that can help you discover what you feel strongly about. And remember, you can control your emotions.

Repeat these words:
I recognize my strong emotions, and I can control my response to those feelings. I express my feelings safely.

Deb Dunham

Sometimes I get pushed around because I'm so shy.

Have you ever been in a group of people who were making fun of someone and you said nothing even though you disagreed with them? Have you ever been convinced to do something you didn't want to do? If so, I bet it didn't feel good.

It feels rotten to be pushed around, but it may not always seem safe to speak up. You may worry that what you want to say will be unpopular or disagreeable. It's often more comfortable for you to keep your thoughts to yourself. But, when you choose not to speak up, you're sending a message to yourself and to the world that your feelings, thoughts, and opinions don't matter—but they do matter. And speaking up can make the difference between getting what you want or not. By expressing your opinion, you might even help someone else who feels the same way but was too shy to speak up.

Sometimes being just an observer is an acceptable choice. But when you feel bullied into actions or words that aren't right for you, it's time to use your voice. That may mean you have to take a risk and step out of your shyness. You might be surprised by the response you get from others. Each time you stand up for yourself by expressing your true feelings, you will become more confident. You will realize that it can feel better to be open than to hide inside of yourself.

Speaking up doesn't mean that your opinions matter more than other people's or that you're always right, but it's your responsibility to be true to yourself. No one can speak your truth better than you. Be brave!

Repeat these words:

I have decided to speak up for myself when I need to. I now choose to be true to myself in thoughts, words, and actions.

Sometimes I feel so sad that I can't stop crying.

Our minds can get so filled up with negativity. Sometimes we don't even know why we're sad, but we definitely feel crummy. When nothing seems to be going right, it's tempting to let the dark thoughts block out the goodness in our lives like dark clouds covering the sun. Sadness is an emotion that can weigh you down and make life seem more difficult than it needs to be. As with other emotions, sadness is normal and needs to be expressed. It's not wise to listen only to the feelings you enjoy.

Crying is one way to relieve sadness. Talking about what makes you sad can also help. Sometimes, just a change of scenery can brighten your mood. Ask yourself if there's anything you can do at this moment to solve your problem. If not, do something different—go outdoors, play with a pet, draw or write—just keep busy. By doing something fun, you aren't ignoring the sadness; you're just taking a break from thinking about it so your body can rest.

Although it's not natural to feel happy all the time, you can change negative emotions to positive ones by changing your thoughts and words. If you feed your sadness with more negative thoughts like, "Things will never get better," the sadness will grow stronger. Negative thoughts like to hang out with other negative thoughts. It's like feeding a stray cat—the cat will want to stick around if it gets the kind of food it wants. On the other hand, if the stray cat shows up and you feed it dog food, it won't want to come around as much. You can feed your own stray cat named "Sadness" positive thoughts like, "I know I can handle this challenge. I'll feel happy again soon." With positive thoughts surrounding it, the sadness won't want to stick around.

Deb Dunham

If after caring for yourself in all of these ways you still feel like the sadness is bigger than you, ask for help from a trusted adult. You deserve to feel happy.

Repeat these words:
I care for myself by respecting all of my feelings.
I wrap my sadness in good thoughts
and I feel good.

Deb Dunham

Sometimes I get so nervous like when I have a test or when I have to speak in front of the class.

Most likely you're nervous because you're afraid that you may not perform well. Did you know that being anxious could actually make you do worse? When you're faced with a situation that makes you nervous, ask yourself, "What will happen if I don't perform as well as I hope?" Can you still be happy that you tried your best? It's okay to do just okay sometimes. The important part is to do your best.

Each time you do something that's difficult for you, take one step at a time instead of focusing on the whole task. Fill your mind with thoughts of success and refuse to think about failing. Give yourself a pat on the back for the things you've done well. Believe in your greatness no matter what the challenge or outcome, and the nervousness will fade. You can do it!

Repeat these words:
I stay relaxed as I fill my mind
with calm, confident, thoughts.
I see a successful me. I can
do anything!

Deb Dunham

Sometimes I feel like I'm dumb.

Do you struggle with one or more subjects in school? Does it seem like everyone knows more than you do? Fear not. You are not dumb! Being smart is about much more than getting good grades and proving how much you know. Smart people are the ones who recognize their own talents and work on strengthening them.

You have so many talents. Some of your talents may still be in hiding, just waiting for you to discover them. If you spend time worrying about what you're not good at, you rob your talents of the attention they need to grow strong. Instead of focusing on the times you feel not good enough, spend more time focusing on things you do well. Maybe you play an instrument or a sport. Are you creative? Do you have a special way with animals? All these examples and more are reasons to feel smart and talented.

Finding your talents can be like searching for buried treasure. Keep your eyes open for your own treasure—the moments you can and do shine. You are a genius—a valuable one!

Repeat these words:
I was given many talents.
I now focus on what I
am good at and on what
I enjoy.

Sometimes I feel so embarrassed like when I tripped and fell getting on the bus and everyone laughed.

I bet that if you ask anyone to name an embarrassing moment, they'd have several to choose from. The human body and mind sometimes slip up, making you do or say something other than what you intended. Instead of letting these moments embarrass you, try to laugh at them. Can you see how it might be funny to watch yourself fall into a bus? You could try making a joke like, "That last step is a doozy!" If others see that you're lighthearted and accepting, they're more likely to react the same way. Most importantly, separate yourself from what happened. A silly action does not mean that you are a silly person.

Repeat these words:
I can laugh at my own blunders. A silly action is just a silly action. I am defined not by my blunders,
but by how I react to them.

Deb Dunham

Sometimes I feel like no one loves me.

You deserve to be loved unconditionally just as you are. Unfortunately, you can't always count on others to provide the love that you need, want, and deserve. You may become disappointed in other people or in yourself.

At times when you're feeling unloved, it is most important to love yourself. Turn off the negative voice in your head—the one that says things like, "There must be something wrong with me. Everyone hates me." This voice is not a friend to you. It doesn't tell the truth. Instead, listen to the voice inside that says, "I'm terrific!" This is the voice you can count on to help you.

It's always a good idea to say nice things to yourself, but it's especially important when you feel low.

Try writing a list of your good qualities and read it to yourself often. You are the most important person in your life. Having a good relationship with yourself is the key to having good relationships with others.

Remember, you are completely lovable just as you are.

Repeat these words:
I am completely lovable just as I am.
I love myself.
I have decided to be kind and gentle
with myself
because I deserve it!

> **Sometimes people tell me I'm too sensitive because I get my feelings hurt really easily. They say I overreact, but I can't help it. So I try to hold my feelings in.**

It's impossible to be "too" anything. Think about the story of *Goldilocks and the Three Bears*. Upon entering the bears' house, Goldilocks first finds a bed that is too hard for her, yet it is great for Papa Bear. Then she finds a bed that is too soft for her, but Mama Bear likes it. Finally, Goldilocks finds Baby Bear's bed that is "just right" for her. Just as there was a different bed to fit each of the different bears and Goldilocks, there are different personalities to fit each unique person. You can't be too sensitive because sensitivity fits you. It's just right for you because it describes part of who you are. And who you are is unique and valuable.

Being sensitive may mean that you cry more than others, or have more hurt feelings, but sensitivity also allows you to hear your own feelings more easily. And feelings have a lot to teach us. Sensitive people often understand things better because they sense problems and possibilities when other, less sensitive, people don't.

Being different from someone else does not mean that you should change. If someone is uncomfortable with your sensitivity, then that person needs to learn to appreciate that differences among people are gifts. If being sensitive means being you, congratulations—that is one of your gifts!

Repeat these words:
Each day I am learning to appreciate myself more.
I see that every person has unique gifts.
One of my gifts is _____.

Deb Dunham

Sometimes I feel bad about myself because I want to be the best at something, but I'm not good at anything. I'm always the last kid picked for a team or a project.

Wouldn't it be nice to be good at everything? Being left out feels rotten. You want to feel wanted and valuable, but you feel worthless. You try your hardest, but you still don't feel like you measure up. Warning! This is the negative voice in your head taking over—the voice that doesn't know the real and magnificent you. It's up to you to turn off this voice. You can do this just like you turn off a radio. Simply refuse to listen. Good, now you need to replace those negative thoughts with positive ones. Fill up your mind with thoughts of your greatness.

If you haven't done it already, make a list of every strength you have. Maybe you're not a star at team sports or group projects, but you *do* shine at many things. Are you a hard worker? Are you organized? Or maybe you're a good listener, a whiz at reading, or a knowledgeable collector. These skills may not be recognized by others in your daily life, and they may not get you picked for a team, but these strengths are important and useful.

It would be nice to be recognized and to feel popular, but it's even better to feel good about the real you. Besides, there's one thing you'll always be better at than someone else—being yourself! No one can do it like you.

Repeat these words:
I remind myself that I shine in many ways.
I love knowing that my talents are
important and useful.

Deb Dunham

Sometimes I feel like I'm always messing up and making bad choices. I can't do anything right.

Life gives us many choices. It takes practice to know how to handle the situations in each new day. If it seems difficult to make wise choices, it may help you to learn some strategies for self-control. Start by noticing the times, places, or situations that are a problem for you. Before speaking or acting, count to ten in your head. This technique helps you to slow down and to think more clearly.

Remember that human beings are not perfect, but we do have the ability to learn from our mistakes. Admitting to and apologizing for the times you have acted poorly can help you move on to better choices.

More importantly, forgive yourself. You're always learning. If you make a mistake, look in a mirror and gently say, "I like you anyway." Never put yourself down—out loud or silently. Instead, praise yourself whenever possible for the things you've done well. For example, instead of saying, "I can't believe I forgot to bring my book home from school again! I have a bad memory," you might say, "I forgot my book today, but I remembered the worksheets. I'll write myself a note next time to help my memory." The point is to try to help yourself instead of beating yourself up. This will help to strengthen your good choices. You're great!

Repeat these words:
Every day, in every way, I am getting better and better.
I forgive myself for my mistakes. I believe I can
make good choices.

Deb Dunham

Sometimes I feel frustrated because I want so many things that I can't have. My parents tell me to be grateful for what I have.

Knowing what you want can be very helpful in getting to know yourself. And wanting something enough can inspire you to take action. For example, if you really want to be a performer when you grown up, you find ways to support that dream. You might take dance lessons, put on shows for friends, and sing whenever you can. This is a

Deb Dunham

positive kind of wanting because it focuses your attention on a possible future career while enjoying yourself now. But then there is the kind of wanting that never satisfies you.

This kind of wanting is like a pig that eats and eats and always wants more. It includes things like wanting the latest toy or electronic device even though you have a similar but older version. This kind of wanting is greedy. Businesses who want you to buy their products know about this greedy wanting. Their advertisements are designed to make you think that you need to have their products in order to be cool, trendy, and happy. It's a big trick—but you're smart enough not to be fooled.

One way to stop the greedy type of wanting is to focus on being thankful. When you focus on what you already have, you'll begin to see that your life is full of treasures— treasures that lose their value only when you forget to be thankful for them. Practice being thankful for one different thing every day. It's easy to think of the big things that you're grateful for like family and friends, but don't forget to appreciate the small ones. For example, practice saying, "I am grateful for the soft feel of pajamas," or "I love the color of my room." You might even start a gratitude bowl. To do this, place a large empty bowl where you'll see it every day. Beside it, place a pen and strips of colorful paper. At least once a day, use one of these papers to write about something you're grateful for. Then place it in the bowl. Soon, your bowl will be overflowing. When you can see all that you have to be thankful for, the urge to have more will get quieter.

Repeat these words:

I recognize wants that are good for me and I patiently wait
to receive them. I am aware of all that I already have
to be grateful for. I add to the happiness in my life
when I am grateful.

Deb Dunham

Sometimes I wish everyone would go away and leave me alone. I don't like to talk about what's bothering me.

How great that you recognize your need for privacy when you feel upset! Everyone needs some time alone with her own uninterrupted thoughts. Spending time alone can help you to sort through your feelings, solve a problem, or simply clean out your mental closet.

Although it is sometimes easier to hide your emotions than it is to talk about them, unexpressed feelings don't just disappear. Instead, they clutter up your insides and eventually make you feel worse. They can even make you sick. Your body has enough work to do without the added stress of carrying around bothersome feelings.

Taking a few deep breaths with your eyes closed while imagining a peaceful place can help you feel better. If you don't feel like talking, try writing or drawing about how you feel. You may want to start a "feelings scrapbook" from your words and pictures. On your pages, you can tell how you felt, why you reacted the way you did, what you wish had happened or not happened, or any information that helps you to feel better. When some time has passed, you can look back at your pages and learn from the feelings you've had. You might even wonder why you felt the way you did or you might see a different way of reacting the next time that feeling pops up. The important part is to take the time to let your feelings out in a healthy way. You deserve to feel good inside and out.

Repeat these words:
I take time by myself to listen to my feelings.
I have many ways to express my feelings.
When I express my feelings, my mind is clear.

> **Sometimes I feel disappointed because no one notices how hard I worked. I was proud of myself and no one else was.**

It sure does feel good to be noticed! Compliments, applause, a pat on the back—any kind of praise—is a nice boost. It can make your achievements seem to double in importance just because someone else noticed. Yet, when you aren't noticed or congratulated, you feel disappointed and deflated—like someone let the air out of your balloon of success. To avoid this feeling, try to think of praise as an extra piece of candy. Being happy and proud of yourself is like eating one big candy bar— delicious and satisfying. Enjoy it. You earned it. If someone else notices your accomplishment, it's like getting a second piece of candy—a bonus even though you were happy with the first piece. You can't always expect the praise of others, but you can expect your own praise. No one can take away your sense of accomplishment unless you let them. That's why it is smarter to work at what makes you feel good about yourself instead of working to impress others. Be your own biggest fan. You're a star!

Repeat these words:

I am proud of my accomplishments even when no one else is. When I do my best, I feel good about my efforts.

Deb Dunham

CHAPTER 2
Feelings about My Family

Sometimes I feel like my parents don't listen to me.

It's frustrating to feel ignored! You have important things to say and deserve to be taken seriously. Parents are busy people with lots of responsibilities, so they don't always recognize your need to be heard. This doesn't mean they don't care. But they may have forgotten that listening is a way of caring.

Sometimes parents have to be reminded to slow down so they can listen better. It's okay to remind your parents that your feelings are important and that you need an adult to care about what you have to say. If your parents don't listen to you or understand you, don't give up. Try again. It may not be the right time for them to do their best listening. Ask them when they might have time to talk without distractions.

Learning to communicate effectively is a skill you can practice that you'll use for the rest of your life. Know what you need and confidently ask for it.

Repeat these words:
I know that I can get the attention I need
by asking for it clearly
and honestly.
Each day I learn
to communicate better.

" Sometimes I think my family is weird. I feel like I don't belong.

At this age, it may not feel good to you to be different. You might worry that people will make fun of you or your family. Or maybe you think that your family just doesn't understand you. Every family and every person is different. That's good news! Wouldn't life be boring if everyone was the same?

Deb Dunham

Try focusing on the positive differences in your family. Even the little things count. What do you appreciate about each person? What do they add to your life that makes it better? How do they help you?

Keeping a sense of humor is a big help in appreciating your family. For example, instead of being embarrassed, could you laugh about how your father sings off-key in front of your friends? Try flipping the situation around. Would you think badly of your friend if *her* father did this? Probably not. Often, the only one judging your family harshly is you!

Being part of a small, special group of people called "family" is the way you learn the skills necessary to be a part of the bigger world. In any kind of family, you learn how to relate to people, how to tolerate differences, and how to be yourself. These are skills you will use for your entire life. However, even in a group, you are a person with an identity of your own. It is possible to be yourself and to live happily with people who are very different from you. No one can change or hide the real you—except you. You can't choose your family, but you can choose what kind of family member you want to be.

Repeat these words:
I now choose to appreciate and accept
the uniqueness of my family.
I am free to be my own person.

> **Sometimes I get annoyed that my parents don't trust me. They're so strict! I wish adults would stop telling me what to do. I can take care of myself.**

Because parents care about their children, they want to protect them from harm and poor choices. That protectiveness may seem like a lack of trust. You might feel that your parents treat you like a baby because they don't let you watch the television programs or movies that you want to watch. Or maybe you think you should be able to stay up late, but your parents disagree.

If you want more freedom to make decisions for yourself, you can begin by showing that you're responsible. Show your parents that you're capable of making responsible choices every day by doing chores without complaining, using good manners without reminders, and dressing appropriately for the weather. Be dependable by doing what you say you will do. If you act in a trust-worthy manner, adults are more likely to agree when you ask for more freedom.

Even when you must listen to instructions, you have a choice: either do it with a smile or fight it. Which seems easier? Which choice earns you more respect?

Today, pay attention to the choices you have in every situation. Promise to make choices that feel good to you and to others. Before you know it, people will start treating you with the new level of trust that you deserve.

Repeat these words:
I am capable and dependable.
I am in the process of earning trust, responsibility,
and independence.

Deb Dunham

Sometimes I think my parents like my brother better than me. He gets all the attention. It's not fair that he never gets in trouble.

You can't judge a tennis match if you're standing only on one side of the court, right? To get a clear view of both sides, you must be standing in the middle. It's the same for you and your siblings. You are standing only on your own side. From your point of view, it may seem that your parents favor your brother. But you aren't in a position to see the whole picture. In reality, your parents probably try very hard to be fair to each of you.

Sometimes, though, parents do give more attention to one of their children than the others. Usually this is because that child needs the attention or asks for it. Siblings who are much younger than you need more attention because they can't do as many things as you can. Sometimes even an older sibling will need more attention because he's struggling with a problem. Instead of keeping track of the amount of attention your siblings get, try noticing your own needs.

Once you're clear about what it is that you want from your parents, try talking to them about how you feel using "I" statements like, "I feel that I get in trouble more than my brother." This works much better than saying, "You treat him better than you treat me." After listening to you, your parents may or may not agree that they have some changes to make. Either way, be willing to listen to them and to accept responsibility for your own actions. If you focus on correcting some of your own behavior, you will waste less time competing with your brother and have more time to practice good communication as a way to fulfill your own needs.

Repeat these words:
I focus on my own relationship with my parents.
I make positive changes in my behavior in order to
have the best life possible.

Deb Dunham

66 **Sometimes it seems like our family fights more than other families.**

Fighting with someone or even listening to others fight is disturbing. When fighting happens in your family, it can make you feel scared, lonely, sad, or confused. You may wonder if your family will break apart because of the fighting. Or you may wonder if your family is abnormal because you don't see other families fighting. Keep in mind that people tend to behave differently when they are with others than when they're in the privacy of their own family. So not seeing something doesn't mean that it doesn't exist.

Still, you have important concerns that have no easy answers. People argue for so many different reasons and expect different results. For example, have you ever argued with your sister because she took something that belonged to you and you wanted it back? On another day, you may have fought with her because she tattled on you and you wanted to defend yourself. Neither argument meant you didn't love your sister just because you were unhappy with her actions at the time. You were angry and decided to speak up about your feelings. However, when you're angry, it's easy to lose control and use words or actions that are hurtful— ones that you often regret. And the more you practice fighting as a way to communicate, the harder it is to change.

You and each of your family members deserve to feel respected and safe no matter what. If you feel unsafe because of the fighting in your home, it's important to talk to an adult that you trust. In this case, it's best to ask for help from someone who is neutral, or not part of your family. Teachers, counselors, and nurses at school are trained to help in this kind of situation. Even if you think you under-stand what's happening at home, remember that adult

Deb Dunham

problems belong to adults, and as a tween, it's not your job to figure them out. Most importantly, know that if your parents fight, it is never your fault.

If safety is not a concern for you at home, and you can discuss with your parents what's bothering you, go for it! By speaking up, you can be a good example and remind others that communicating respectfully without hurtful insults is important for healthy relationships.

Repeat these words:
I do my best to communicate respectfully.
I deserve to feel respected and safe
at all times.

> **Sometimes I feel like my parents are always criticizing me and telling me what I do wrong. I feel like I can't do anything right.**

Adults, like young people, are not perfect. They sometimes make poor choices by choosing words that hurt more than they help. If the adults in your life choose to criticize you instead of encourage you, it is their mistake. It doesn't mean that they're bad people or that you are bad.

Adults may not even realize how their words and actions make you feel. But you can help others to understand you by being truthful about how you feel. Using statements that begin with "I" is a good way to communicate your feelings. For example, try saying, "I feel terrible when you criticize me. I'm sorry I made that mistake. I'd like to make it right. I need help but I feel like I'm bothering you." That sounds better than, "Why are you so mean? You're always yelling at me. You treat me like you don't want me around."

There's nothing wrong with reminding your parents that you're always trying your best and that if they encourage you, it will help you much more than if they criticize you. You have the right to make mistakes, and your parents do, too!

Repeat these words:
I know that I am a good person.
I know that approving of myself
is important.

Deb Dunham

CHAPTER 3
Feelings about My Friends

Sometimes I get so jealous of other people who have what I want.

Paying attention to the accomplishments and possessions of others is one way to get motivated to set goals for your own life. But when you focus on what you don't have, jealousy can creep in and make you feel and act in ways that you don't like. When someone has something that you wish was yours—a toy, a skill, or a friend—it's hard not to be jealous. However, just as you want the best for yourself, it's equally important to want the best for others. Think about it: when you have what someone else wants, doesn't it feel better when they are happy for you?

By setting goals for yourself and competing only with yourself, you are more likely to feel satisfied. One way to help you move in the right direction is to create a list or a collage of your dreams and goals and hang it in your room for motivation. Look at it every day and say, "I intend to _____(add your goal)_____."

Easier to say than to do, right? Try these tricks to shift your focus: Imagine your success often. Feel the feelings you'll have when you reach your goal. Concentrate on your own achievements, however small, and be proud of them. See yourself receiving what you want. Doing all of these things will help jealousy to fade away because you will be focusing positive thoughts on yourself. And remember, positive thoughts attract positive changes!

Repeat these words:
I am in the process of achieving my own goals and dreams.
Just for now, I've decided to be happy for others, too.

" Sometimes people are so mean.

Every expression of unkindness starts from fear or ignorance. Often people are unkind because they are hurting inside. If someone has been treated badly, she may not feel good about herself. Bullies may be scared people who want to scare others. They may be jealous of you. It's as if they want to share their pain with others as a way to make themselves feel better. Understanding that this is possible does not make their actions okay. But once you understand meanness, you may be able to react to it better.

If you've responded to meanness with your own meanness, you know that it did little or nothing to help the situation. Often, simply ignoring another person's poor choice of behavior will stop it. Sometimes responding with humor will weaken a bully. But if you ever feel that you're unsafe because of bullying, you may need the help of an adult. In any case, you do not have to tolerate unkind words or behavior. You have the right to be respected. It's not your job to change how other people act, but it is your job to protect yourself. Expect and insist on kindness from yourself and from others.

In addition to protecting your body, it's equally important to protect your feelings from injury. How? With a positive self-image. Imagine that your whole inner self is a castle. This castle is so valuable, that it's protected by an invisible shield—the shield of self-respect. This shield is made up of all your beliefs about yourself. The more positive your beliefs about yourself are, the stronger the shield is. Words that strengthen your shield could be, "I am courageous." "I am a very important person." "I love myself." "I deserve to be treated well." With these thoughts and beliefs, the words that are meant to harm you can more easily

Deb Dunham

bounce off of you. Having self-respect means knowing that you deserve to be treated well by everyone.

Repeat these words:
I respect myself and expect others to do the same.
I like knowing that I am a
worthwhile person.

Deb Dunham

" Sometimes I feel bad about myself because the boy that I like doesn't like me back.

When someone you like doesn't feel the same way about you, it is tempting to feel bad about yourself. You may wonder what's wrong with you or even try to change how you look or behave. Don't do it! Here's an example of why wishing to be different is never the best choice.

Imagine for a minute that you have a magic wand. You have decided that if you were a tall, athletic, blue-eyed girl with a small nose, then you would be attractive to all the best people. Then one day, you meet a boy that you like very much. He seems perfect for you, but he doesn't return the affection. "Why don't you like me?" you ask. He answers, "You're very nice, but I prefer shorter girls with dark skin and larger facial features. And I'm not very interested in sports." Surprise! He prefers the kind of girl you used to be before you decided that you needed to change.

While it is natural to hope that certain people prefer to be with you, you have no power to change another person's feelings. It's like asking someone to like the color blue when they prefer red. Both choices are beautiful, but they are not the same. Trust that you will connect with the people you are meant to be with.

Try to love yourself, especially when you're feeling rejected. When you love yourself, you send a message to the world that says, "I accept that I am attractive and great to be with." Loving and accepting yourself are signs of true inner strength. And true inner strength is what really matters.

Repeat these words:
I see that I am attractive and great to be with. I choose to love and accept myself so others can, too.

Deb Dunham

Sometimes I feel like I can't trust anyone. I told my friend a secret and she told a bunch of kids at school. I feel terrible.

It's very disappointing when friends disrespect you by repeating private conversations without your permission. It might even feel like the whole world knows your business. Even though your friend thinks it's no big deal, you still feel cheated and hurt. Now you wonder whom you can trust.

For starters, you can always recognize a fake friend if she tells other people's secrets to you, or gossips about her other friends. You can be sure she would do the same to you. This is a person you can't trust, a person who is only interested in herself.

On the other hand, a good friend knows the importance of being loyal at all times. She tries to help you and never puts you down. She also doesn't decide to be your friend on some days and not on others. When you're with true friends, you feel happy. It feels safe to be yourself because you're not worried that your friend will think you're weird. And, of course, you have fun together.

The best way to attract good friends into your life is by being a good friend. Be honest, sincere, dependable, and kind. Listen as much as you talk, and be happy for your friends' successes. Most importantly, remember to be your own best friend. Be the person you can always count on. You deserve good friends. Don't settle for less!

> **Repeat these words:**
> I deserve good friends.
> Being trustworthy is important to me.
> I surround myself with people
> who care about me.

Sometimes I feel sad when old friends change and decide they don't like me anymore.

It's okay to let yourself be sad at the loss of a friend's affection. It's like saying goodbye to a favorite old sweatshirt that doesn't fit anymore. You hate to see it go, but you know that you can't keep it. Besides, if you tried to keep all the things and people you cherish, you would never have room for new ones. Maybe there's a new friend who has been waiting for a spot to open up in your life.

While you're waiting for an opportunity to make a new friend, remember to be a good friend to yourself. It's okay to feel sad about a loss, but it's not okay to let the loss make you feel bad about yourself or your life. To combat the sadness, do something fun by yourself. Being your own best friend is good medicine for a heartache and will help you to feel happy again.

Repeat these words:
Today I choose to see myself in positive ways.
I am my own best friend. I enjoy my own company
and others do, too.

Deb Dunham

CHAPTER 4
Feelings about My Life and the World

Sometimes I get so disappointed when things don't work out the way I want them to.

Things don't always work out according to our plans, but they always work out for the best. This is an idea that may be hard to accept, but experience will show you that it's true. For example, have you ever been disappointed by a shopping trip in which you found the "perfect outfit" but couldn't find it in your size? Then, on your next shopping trip you found an even better outfit that was not only your size, but also less expensive?

You never know how a disappointment will affect your life. It may be good luck in disguise. Instead of letting disappointment get you down, tell yourself that everything is just as it should be. Trust that all will work out for the best. Then keep your eyes open for a good turn of events.

Repeat these words:
All is well. I am happier when
I remember that even
disappointments work
out for the best.

Deb Dunham

> **Sometimes I feel like I don't want to try new things or play games because I hate to fail or to lose.**

Everyone of every age makes mistakes. Failing or losing can feel horrible. But it can also be the best way to learn. If you try to avoid failure by not participating in life, you may be missing out on a lot of fun.

When you do lose or fail at something, it's okay to be disappointed. Just remember to give yourself a pat on the back for the things you did well. Congratulate yourself for trying and never lose hope that you can do better. Successful people accept that they won't always win, and they keep on trying anyway!

Repeat these words:
Trying is worth celebrating.
I have decided to participate fully in life.
I allow myself to learn from mistakes.

Deb Dunham

Sometimes I don't know who to be or how to act so that people will like me. I just don't fit in.

The world is a huge place with billions of people in it. By this age, you have probably experienced only a small piece of this huge planet. You may feel like you don't fit in now, but as you grow, your life expands and you will find more places, experiences, and people to connect with. As you work on accepting yourself, be willing to tolerate differences in those around you. You don't have to be the same as someone else in order to get along with her. You may find a great friend in a person who is very different from you.

There is only one you and you are special! The world needs you to be yourself. It's your job, your gift to the world, to work on being yourself. The good news is that you already know all you need to know to be yourself at this moment. When you feel confused about how to act, it may be because you're trying to imitate someone else. Spending some time alone can help you to climb back into your own skin. Remember, you can only be your *best* self when you *are* yourself. Wouldn't you rather be a good version of you, than a bad version of someone else?

The secret to fitting in is to accept yourself. Remind yourself that you have a special place in this world reserved just for you. We are all like pieces of a huge puzzle. It sometimes takes a while to figure out where you fit into that puzzle, but you can be sure that you do fit! And without you or me or any other person, the puzzle would be incomplete.

Repeat these words:

I am the best at being me. Just for today, no matter what happens, I decide to really like being me.

Deb Dunham   TWEEN YOU & ME 43

> **Sometimes I hear scary stories and I worry about bad things happening to me or to the people I love. I feel like I'm afraid of everything.**

The world can seem like a scary place. It's hard to make sense of all the stories you hear. Sometimes you hear stories from friends, grown-ups, television, or the radio that are scary. Your mind can run away with an idea that isn't true. When this happens you may mistakenly think those scary things happen frequently and that they happen nearby. But frightening stories have a way of spreading. The incidents could have happened far away from you. Or maybe the story has been exaggerated as it was passed along. You can't believe everything you hear, but you can protect yourself from being scared unnecessarily by walking away and refusing to listen to scary stories or the news, which is meant for adult ears.

Although you can protect yourself from unnecessary fear in this way, know that fear is not an emotion you want to ignore. Fear is a gift you were born with that protects you from danger. It's like your personal guard dog that wants you to be safe so it alerts you to danger. Fear is a loyal friend who will be with you even as an adult. However, fear can get carried away if you aren't paying attention. Just as a guard dog would wander out of your yard if it wasn't leashed or fenced in, fear will wander if your mind lets it.

When you're afraid, you need to ask yourself, "What is true and what is my fear making up?" For instance, you feel afraid of the dark but ask yourself, "Is there really anything in the dark that wasn't there in the light? Or is my fear creating stories?" Sometimes it helps to ask other people who don't have the same fears

Deb Dunham

as you do why they aren't afraid. If you know why others feel safe, it may help you to see things differently.

On the other hand, you need to pay attention to your fear when it's trying to protect you from real danger. For example, if someone tried to get you to jump down a whole flight of stairs, your fear would say, "No way! That would hurt me. This person is not interested in my safety." And you would listen to your fear because your whole body and mind agree that this fear is real.

Your experiences will make you more confident in recognizing the difference between fear that protects you from danger and fear that needs to be leashed. Respect your fears and promise yourself that you will work at sorting them out.

Repeat these words:
I know when my fear is warning me of real danger.
I am learning to trust my feelings and
listen to them. I deserve to feel safe and secure.
I can tell someone if I am afraid.

Deb Dunham

Sometimes I worry about growing up. What should I be?

Every day you become a new version of yourself. You can't possibly know what the future holds for you. You can only choose to follow your heart in this moment. Start paying attention to the times you feel most free. What activities could you do for hours and not get bored? When do you feel most capable and confident? The answers to these questions are messages from your heart and from the true you. Listen to these clues as you grow.

When you're faced with any important decision, close your eyes and pay attention to how you feel inside. Make decisions based on what feels good inside. This is called "trusting your gut." If you listen to the positive voice inside yourself, the path to the future will be clear. You can and will make a difference in the world. Take one step at a time. You're on the right track!

Repeat these words:
I am filled with excitement about the person I am becoming.
My possibilities are endless.
I am building a great life for myself.

Deb Dunham

Sometimes I feel excited about moving to a new town and a new school, but mostly I feel sad, lonely, and scared.

Why wouldn't you feel all these emotions? Moving into new situations is very emotional. Even if you're excited, you can't help but wonder how different your life may be at your new location. With so many changes, it helps to spend time thinking about all of the things that will stay the same. Is your family moving with you? Your pet? Your favorite toys? What are some new and positive changes? I bet you can't even imagine all of the great possibilities that will show up in time.

If your parents haven't already thought of it, you could suggest some helpful transitional steps like hosting a going-away party in which you exchange photos or scrapbooks. Or if someone wants to give you a going-away present, suggest a phone card so you can contact your friends. In addition to talking about how you feel, you could write a story about what you hope your new life will be like. Then read it to yourself over and over.

You *can* survive a big move and even enjoy it if you stay open to this new adventure. Decide that change is good and it will be true.

Repeat these words:
I have decided to be open to new experiences.
I thrive in any situation.
I imagine a great life
for myself.

Sometimes I feel like my life stinks. I want so many things that I can't have. My parents tell me to stop complaining and to be grateful for what I have.

Of course you want to complain when things don't go your way. But complaining and blaming are so destructive. Complaining about the things you can't change makes it harder for everyone. When you find yourself complaining, *stop* and ask yourself, "Is there anything I can do to change this situation?" If you think of a positive solution, try it! If your solution involves others, suggest your ideas. If you can't think of a solution right away, don't worry. It may come to you later when you're less emotional.

Choosing to complain or to blame someone else for your situation is like trying to walk through a wall. Turn away from that wall of complaints, and positive ideas and changes will appear. You will find that people are much more willing to work with you if you focus on a solution rather than complain about a problem.

Repeat these words:
I have the ability to improve my life with positive thinking and positive behavior. When I let go of complaining, I can focus on solutions rather than problems.

Deb Dunham

Sometimes I feel so alone—like there's no one in the world who understands my problems.

Growing up means big changes. It isn't unusual to feel frightened and alone during this time. But this is a big world—you are not alone. Many young people are facing the same problems that you are. You may not realize it if they don't talk about it. And, there are so many people who want to support you and help you to be happy. You don't have to figure out all your problems alone. Sharing your struggles with a trusted adult—a parent, friend, teacher, nurse, counselor, or coach—can help to relieve the stress of growing up and lessen the feelings of aloneness.

Finding someone you can talk to about your feelings is the first step. Willingness to express your feelings is the next step. Do yourself the favor of speaking up, even if it is difficult for you. When you open up to someone about how you feel, you may be surprised to find out that they truly do understand what you're going through. Knowing that you aren't alone is sometimes all you need to feel better.

Repeat these words:
I realize that I am not alone in this life. I feel better when I share my feelings with people I trust.

Deb Dunham   TWEEN YOU & ME 49

Sometimes life is so hard!

Yes, life can be hard! Often, you're faced with challenges that require a lot of strength and courage. You may wonder when life will get easier. The truth is that as long as you live, you'll be faced with new experiences that challenge you. The good news is that each time you overcome a difficulty, you gain more confidence in your ability to handle the next challenge. Whenever you're tempted to focus on how hard a situation is, try seeing it as an opportunity instead. Chances are, this challenge is an opportunity for you to become a better, stronger, or smarter version of you.

Think of the time when you were younger and learning to tie your shoes. It seemed so difficult then. Now that you've grown, you may wonder why you thought it was so hard. There are hundreds of examples like this one that show you how often you've conquered a challenge.

You have tremendous strength within you. That inner strength is always there when you need it. Believe in your own power to face the challenges in your life.

Repeat these words:
I have a huge amount of inner strength
to deal with the challenges of life.
I now see challenges as opportunities
to learn about myself.
I see a courageous and
confident me.

Deb Dunham

Sometimes I feel like I'm cursed. Bad things always happen to me.

If you feel like a black cloud is following you, take heart. It's not true. In reality, you're probably not experiencing any more bad luck than the next person, but you may be giving all your attention to the events you don't want in your life. A very simple and effective way to rid yourself of this cursed feeling is to refuse to let this thought stay in your mind. Each time you're tempted to think or say that you're unlucky, replace that thought with, "So many good things happen to me." Then picture good things that have happened, or that you'd like to happen. When you fill your mind with positive thoughts, you will begin to notice positive changes. More of what you like, want, and appreciate will come into your life. That is the power of positive thinking!

Repeat these words:
My positive thoughts can change my life for the better.
So many good things happen to me.

> **Sometimes I feel like no one understands me, like when people laugh because they think I'm kidding, but I'm really serious.**

Good communication can be tricky. Misunderstandings happen all the time. Even when you're speaking the same language as someone else, you may not be understood. You feel like you're being clear. What you say makes perfect sense to you. Yet people still don't "get it."

Communication involves much more than just the words we say. Equally important are body language, tone of voice, facial expressions, timing, listening, cultural differences, personal experiences, and opinions. Each of these things matters in conversation. With so much going on, it's no wonder we often misunderstand each other!

The best you can do to be understood is to speak clearly and honestly. If you need to, repeat what's on your mind in a new way. Although others won't always agree with your statements, it is important that they understand your intention—or what you want to communicate— because your words stay with a person long after you've parted.

Repeat these words:
My words are important and valuable. I work at communicating well with others.

PLEASE TAKE ME HOME

Deb Dunham

CONCLUSION

You and Your Choices

I hope that after reading this book and using positive self-talk, you feel even better about yourself and your life. Your life belongs to you. Every moment of it counts. The best part about life is that you get to choose who you are—even as a tween.

You have so many choices. You choose your thoughts, actions, friends, attitudes, and words. All of these choices define who you are. What do your choices say to the world about you?

All people make choices about what kind of person they will be. Even adults struggle with many of the same challenges that you do. As you move through your life, look for people of all ages who make good choices. Watch how their choices affect their lives and the lives of others. While it's not recommended to try to be just like someone else, it is important to have role models to learn from.

Role models can be your parents, other family members, sports figures, teachers, friends, or even strangers. Anyone who sets a positive example can be a good role model. As you admire the qualities in others that make them great people, consider trying those things on for size. Figuring out who you are is like shopping for clothes—it takes practice to know what fits and what style is best for you. Expect to try on lots of clothes, or versions of you, before you find a favorite style. Whatever style you're wearing now, wear it with confidence as you step into the world ready to be the best you.

The most important and courageous choice you could make each day is to love yourself no matter what. You can find lots of things about yourself that make you feel good. Even when your life seems different than you want it to be, you can choose to look in the mirror each day and say, "I see a me who cares for herself, follows her dreams, is courageous, and is learning to accept herself." Choosing to love yourself will not only keep you strong and healthy inside and out, but it also will help you to see the good in the rest of the world, even when the challenges make it look dim. When you love yourself you develop the kind of true inner strength that lets you be who you really want to be in every situation.

You are a powerful force in this world, capable of becoming anything you believe. Start by believing in *you*. You are capable of meeting all of life's challenges. You are a gift to the world! So enjoy your awesome self. I believe in you!

Deb Dunham

APPENDIX

How to Write Your Own Affirmations

Affirmations are statements you make about yourself or about a situation. When you affirm something, you are saying, "This is true." An affirmation can be positive or negative, helpful or hurtful. For example, "I am so bad at math. I'll never get it." (negative) or "I am a great reader." (positive). You can easily see which statement brings you down and which one builds you up.

The goal is to use positive statements as much as possible. This is easy to do when you believe in the truth of your words. If you know you are a great reader, it's easy to say so. On the other hand, if you know you don't do well in math class because your grades are low, it would be hard to tell yourself that you understand math. But this doesn't mean that you can't find a true, positive statement to build your confidence about math. Try these statements:

"I work at math so that I can understand it." "Math is just numbers, and I know numbers." "There are lots of people who can help me understand math."

In these examples, you have changed a negative attitude about a situation into a positive statement that is believable. If you were to focus on these positive affirmations over and over, you would start to feel better about math, which would probably change some of your actions, habits, or behaviors. These changes could improve your performance in math and ultimately improve your grade in this subject. At the very least, you would feel calmer about math and better about yourself for being positive instead of criticizing yourself. And feeling good about yourself is important!

Because what you think of yourself is what you will become.

Here's what you need to know about creating your own positive statements:

What do I want? (Be specific.)

Who is it happening to? (me)

When is it happening? (now)

How does it make me feel? (Great! Be positive.)

Now that you know how to change your self-talk to help you, look for something in your life that you want to improve. Some suggestions are friendships, abilities at school or in sports, or the way you feel about yourself. Once you've thought of the situation and attitude you want to work on, decide exactly what change you'd like to see. Then, write a positive statement about it. Remember to focus on what you want, not what you don't want. Avoid using the words *don't*, *not*, and *no*. For example, avoid saying, "I don't want to be sick." Instead you could say, "My body is healing."

Some situations are harder than others. If you get stuck for the right words, you can always use this for a start: "I see a me who…"

The possibilities are endless. Believe in you!

Get a Journal!
The *Tween You & Me Journal* is available too!

Visit our blog:
www.tweenyouandmebook.com

Acknowledgments

A special thank you to my tween friends who participated in the research portion of this book. Thank you Maya Ambrose, Emily Dunham, Claire Faddis, Rachel Hutter, and Maeve Noonan for your honesty and insights.

I am grateful to Joan Borgatti, a writing coach whose professionalism, expertise, and compassion are equally superb and generously shared.

Nancy Cleary is a rare gem in publishing. Thank you for enthusiastically embracing this project as both a publisher and a mom.

To my friends and family, whose support can never be measured, thank you for letting my passion spill into your lives. You are infinitely patient cheerleaders. Thank you for selflessly wanting this book to succeed and for continually throwing new ideas in my direction.

From the first moment I mentioned the idea for this book, my daughter, Emily adopted this project. Thank you for your ideas about content, your self-initiated marketing efforts, and most of all, your positive encouragement. You are wise beyond your years.

A special thanks to Ben who gently informed me that boys need a different kind of book. Your honesty and wit keep me laughing.

Olivia, not yet a tween, was the one who motivated me to pick up my pen and write when she mistakenly said at 3 years old, "This is your last birthday, Mama."

For as long as I can remember, my parents, Dan and Vera, saw me as supremely competent. Thank you for motivating me to reach for your inflated vision of me.

Note to Parents

If a child is to thrive in her lifetime, she must have a solid sense of her own self-worth. When a child believes that she is capable of facing life's challenges and that her contributions are valued and significant, she can operate from a position of high self-esteem.

In years past, tweens, ages eight to twelve, were presumed to coast between the formative early years and the tumultuous teen years. But now young people, especially girls, are being confronted with mature concerns at an accelerated pace. Without the emotional maturity to process these issues, stress escalates and self-esteem suffers. Children with compromised self-esteem are more likely to engage in risky behaviors, have eating disorders, and suffer socially and emotionally.

Every child could enjoy the benefits of high self-esteem including resiliency, emotional well-being, a sense of personal success, and self-confidence. Yet the prevalence of low self-esteem in preadolescent and adolescent girls is concerning.

So what makes the difference in a child's life? How does one child achieve empowerment and another suffer from the stress of life? In exploring the answers to these questions, we need to realize that self-esteem is not a gift that can be given to children. And once acquired, it can never be taken away. Rather, it is the gradual, reinforced adoption of positive beliefs about one's own capabilities and value. This empowered self-perception can vacillate in strength and vary from one situation to the next. In other words, a child who has an apparently low self-esteem in school and other peer situations can demonstrate high self-esteem while engaging in horseback riding.

Every moment of a child's life provides an opportunity to enhance or detract from her self-esteem. The way a child is treated by the people who are important to her can raise or lower the child's self-esteem. The bottom line—children need to know that they are loved and valued by those who care for them.

Tweens have a particular need for guidance as they begin to absorb the opinions of the world over their own definitions of themselves. Fortunately, they also possess receptivity to positive input that can be captured before it dwindles in the peak of adolescence. You may be surprised to know that tweens actually consider their family to be their preferred source for practical, reliable support. As an adult role model, you are in a perfect position to nourish the self-esteem of your child. The best way to foster qualities of inner strength is to be an example of empowerment. Here are some suggestions:

- Let your child see you make mistakes, accept your fallibility, and rise up from failure. Emphasize the ability to cope with defeat rather than focusing on constant success.

- Be willing to express and share your own true feelings. In doing so, you demonstrate self-acceptance and the importance of emotional self-care.

- Practice positivity. Catch your own negative language and work on transforming it. Avoid put-downs of yourself and others.

- Demonstrate an attitude of ownership for your own choices and behaviors. Adults make mistakes, too. The rules of conduct, including apologies, apply to adults and children alike.

- Encourage yourself and your child to take advantage of new and challenging opportunities, building confidence with each experience.

- Invite a child to share her current concerns and future dreams, and invite her to listen to yours.

- Focus on the fact that we all have choices in every situation, and there-fore, have the capacity to change our environments.

- Above all, treat yourself and your child with respect. By treating her respectfully, you give your daughter the message that she is valuable and deserves to be respected by others. Therefore, she'll be less likely to tolerate mistreatment in her relationships.

Tween You and Me provides an opportunity for meaningful dialogue with your daughter about the many challenges she faces. Most tween girls want and need to speak out, but many won't initiate conver-sation. Imagine your daughter's relief and gratitude to find the support and information she craves in the understanding environment of her family.

It is my hope that many young people and the adults who care for them will find comfort in this book and be inspired toward a life in which all emotions become friends and teachers. With a deeper self-awareness, tweens can bring forth their own inner strength and become the extraordinary people they are meant to be.

CPSIA information can be obtained
at www.ICGtesting.com
Printed in the USA
LVIW021021100413
328511LV00001B

* 9 7 8 0 9 8 2 0 5 1 8 5 6 *